Management Poems by Madhoo

Vol. III

Strategy

#1 – One with All

Strategy in passing,

Leaves many a trace,

For new ones to follow,

And old ones to grace,

Goals change but mean same,

Strategy means same but changes name,

As for planning, implementing or changing,

In finance, marketing or operating,

Strategy works as one with all.

#2 - What is Strategy?

Simple Tactic Ruling A Time in Enterprise Gaming on Years

Simple because it answers a question,

How to increase revenues,

Strategy is to sell more,

Tactic because it needs to tell how,

Sell more by getting more customers,

Ruling because it dominates other priorities,

Just get more buyers, where and when don't matter,

A because it's for a single firm, goal, time,

Time because strategy changes with time,

Enterprise or firm or company uses it most,

Gaming because competitors can win else,

Years pass and strategy needs to work to win.

#3 - Haiku

Seasonal

A strategy changes game

The industry phase is now growing

Its firms are flourishing.

#4 - Strategy Quatrains

Seven of the companies collide,

To merge or not, for markets to decide,

In the game theory, choosing win-win,

For all with profits to grin.

One is a metal firm,

One is a distributor,

One is an assembler,

One is a buyer.

One is a packager,

One is a consultant,

One is a processor,

Teaming up with deals pertinent.

Savings internal, expenses internal,

Losses and profits to remain,

In the strategic group to dwindle,

May be a strategic cluster in vain.

But they all run to find the end-user,

You and I will be their customers,

But as we wonder,

Strategy is a jigsaw for years.

That takes shapes like a wax saw,

Sometimes cutting through the profits,

Sometimes adding to the coffers in
awe,

Companies say that the strategy fits.

5 - Cinquain

Strategy

Long-term, Short-term,

Winning, Changing, Losing,

Restructuring excitement – mergers & acquisitions!

Strategy.

#6 - Hexaplet

In the markets or industries or
companies,

Amongst industries, companies or
employees,

With governments, regulators or
customers,

To get approvals, compliance or sales,

All yearn to reach the day,

Strategies march on the way.

7 - Diamante

Goal

Strategy

Strategic Planning

Strategic Planning & Implementation

Tactical Planning

Tactics

End

8 – Strategy Acrostic

Shines

Through

Rampant

Activities

That

Entangle

Goals

Yearly

9 – Diamante

Sell

A product

In A new market

Too Few new customers

To make those extra revenues

That can cover those rising expenses and wastes

What about those defectives, with defects, damages and lost ones

Not just products but flailing markets and customers

To increase loyalty, reliability, trust

To make new offerings

Word-of-mouth

Be Positive

Strategy

10 – Change Strategy

Change employees

Change technologies

Change products

Change functions

Change tactics

Change services

Change channels

Change dealers

Change distributors

Change partners

Implement Change Strategy

Change Company

Merge with others

Collaborate with rivals

Ally with users

Change customer perception.

11 - Business begins and ends with Strategy

Business is Begetting Umbrella Success with Innovative Networking between Enterprise & Strategic Success

Strategy prevails if strategic gains are visible.

Strategic Gains are visible if strategy implementation is effective.

Strategy implementation is effective if strategy action steps are clear.

Strategy action is clear if strategic planning is complete.

Strategic Planning is complete if strategic horizon is visible.

Strategic horizon is visible if the business problem is clear.

Business problem is clear if the business understanding is complete.

Business understanding is complete if the best strategists are present.

12- Sometimes companies need Strategy to

Run the company

Produce goods

Attract markets

Garner buyers

Create loyalty

Retain customers

Sell the goods

Provide services

Manage distribution

Manage supply-chain

Beat competitors

Manage hierarchies

Operate globally

13

Strategy needs

Business intelligence

Sense-making

Quick decision-making

Change approvers

Wise investment

Cost-benefit analysis

To understand competitors

Market research

Smart planners

Active implementers

Patient leaders

Astute auditors

14

Optimum Strategy gives

Quality excellence

World Standards

Best products

Excellent services

Transformational leaders

New industry benchmarks

New industry standards

Effective managers

Sustained success

Employee satisfaction

Customer delight

Vendor loyalty

Competitor co-optation

15 – Strategy lives on

Employees change, goals change,

Theories change, economies change,

Governments change, rules change,

Customers change, markets change,

Industries change, firms change,

Resources change, capabilities change,

Returns change, interest rates change,

Yields change, stakeholders change,

Investors change, locations change,

Competitors change, partners change,

Strategy lives through all.

16 – Marketing Strategy

Study the buyers,

Understand the users,

Know the customers,

Gauge the consumers,

Drill the employees,

Train the workers,

Set the targets,

Grind the appraisals,

Hunch the competitors,

React to rivals,

Be proactive with markets,

Form the leaders,

Use the partners,

Learn the technologies,

Promote the products,

Hail the qualities,

Repair the errors,

Promise the better,

Give the best,

Then take rest.

17 – Leadership Strategy

Hire the best,

Train the rest,

Cover the levels,

Without dishevels,

Communicate to all,

Respond to all,

Keep the calm,

Don't take the harm,

Make the decisions,

In all situations,

Take the lead,

Follow in need,

Compete with yourself,

Don't be an elf,

Involve other's interests,

Cool the worker unrests,

Talk to competitors,

Don't ignore predators,

Be a dictator,

Against the alligator,

If it does matter,

Stand but not shatter,

Create the markets,

Without any rackets,

Make relationships,

With trust that grips,

Make networks,

Like the bulwarks,

With groups strategic,

And clusters strategic,

Hail the employer company,

Don't blame the rival company,

Protect the firm in tough times,

Be patient in rough times,

Set to motivate,

But do not berate.

18 – Financial Strategy

Invest capital,

Expect returns,

Watch yields,

Monitor interest rates,

Act on time,

To avoid loss chime,

Compare values,

Reduce expenses,

Increase revenues,

Buy low,

Sell high,

Target profits,

Share dividends,

Retain earnings,

Manage leverage,

Collect goodwill,

Intangible is money-in-stock,

Pay employees well,

Don't tax buyers,

Get stocks to high,

Manage exchange rates,

Accumulate & Distribute.

19 – Organizational Strategy

Focus or Diversify

Do not ignore inertia

Note rivals' steps,

Target market shares,

Aim at high sales,

Achieve the robust quality,

Maintain factory premises.

Dance to buyer tunes,

Forget agonies in dunes,

Master the operations,

Work with all levels,

Respect all employees,

Reward all workers,

Satisfy all customers.

Share with the community,

Contribute to the society.

20

Customer Relationship Strategy

Hail customers,

Retain customers,

With positive word-of-mouth,

To prevent sales going south,

Increase loyalty,

Create royalty,

Share with buyers,

Discounts or offers in tiers.

Sell with mind,

Serve with heart,

Understand users,

Reward customers,

Negotiate on preferences,

Resolve doubts,

Meet needs,

Exceed expectations.

Price low,

Sell now,

Sell products,

Offer services,

Provide maintenance,

Guarantee support,

Don't expect support,

Teach use.

Teach technologies,

Learn from customer,

On unknown and new,

Don't ignore customers,

Don't ignore concerns,

Ignore reprimands,

Ignore bad experiences,

Ignore misunderstandings.

Don't take on customers,

But appease customers,

Misery if as it extends,

Remind buyer in mends,

That you are seller,

And not a slave,

Buyer is the strategist,

Seller is the implementer.

21 – Definition of Strategy

Strategy is the way of playing the game abiding by the rules.

Game of competing, rules of competition,

Game of business, rules of industry,

Game of business, rules of nation,

Game of production, rules of company,

Game of excellence, rules of business,

Game of selling, rules of customers,

Game of operations, rules of market...

22 – People Management Strategy

Human resources are tangible,

With strategies that are intangible,

Some like to work in teams,

Some work best on own,

Some like to blame on teams,

Some like to volunteer and own up,

Hire the best,

Pay the best,

Train all,

Reward all,

Promote the better,

Lead the best,

Lead the worst,

Make the leaders,

Make the employees.

Evaluate the skills,

Value the skills,

Build trust,

Enhance reliability,

Promote satisfaction,

As you know appraise,

Not like school progress,

Appreciate to be.

23 – Adamant Strategy

Strategy is adamant if it ignores

People...employees, customers, stakeholders, participants,

Processes...technological, standard, managerial, symbiotic,

Functions...product, business,

Competitors...vendors, suppliers, dealers, partners, allies, players,

Markets...local, global,

Industries...substitute, complementary,

And nations...domestic & foreign.

24 – Strategeables

Strategy should be flexible,

Adaptable ...to environmental needs,

Adoptable ...by business,

Timed ...to market...in timetable,

Actionable ...by employees,

Measurable ...by company,

Implementable ...by managers,

and recognizable ...by customers.

25 – Strategy & Knowledge

Strategy

uses knowledge,

disburses knowledge,

shares knowledge,

depends upon knowledge,

accumulates knowledge,

redirects knowledge,

stores knowledge,

levitates knowledge,

and reuses knowledge.

Madhoo is a Doctor of Philosophy in Strategic Management.